The
KING'S
DECREE

The Power of Speaking the Word of God
Over your Life and Circumstances

MICHAEL VAN VLYMEN

ISBN 978-1-948680-12-7

TO THEM THAT BELIEVE

This is the Power of God to Them that Believe

(As it is written, I have made thee a father of many nations,) before him whom he believed, even God, who quickeneth the dead, and calleth those things which be not as though they were. (Romans 4:17 KJV)

God calls those things that are not as though they were. Why? Because He is changing the reality by the word He speaks. When Jesus told everyone "the girl is not dead but only sleeping", everyone laughed.

He said unto them, Give place: for the maid is not dead, but sleepeth. And they laughed him to scorn. (Matthew 9:24 KJV) People are still laughing today but the reality is that this is the God we serve, the God that makes all things possible and He has also given us an overwhelming promise and instruction.

"Most assuredly, I say to you, he who believes in Me, the works that I do he will do also; and greater works than these he will do, because I go to My Father. (John 14:12 NKJV)

Speaking the word of God is powerful.

CONTENTS

INTRODUCTION

Why I believe in the Power of our Words

One night several years ago during my prayer time, an evil spirit appeared and stood glaring at me in my room. I was in the process of rebuking this evil spirit and commanding him to leave but I was not having much success. Even though I had known about and practiced spiritual warfare for several years and I knew I was seated in authority in Christ, this spirit would not budge. I tried every way I knew to make him leave but not only did he not leave but he appeared as if my words had absolutely no effect on him. I rebuked him for fully twenty minutes before he finally left and I was more than a bit perplexed as to how this could happen.

After this encounter I went to the Lord and asked him, "Lord, how can this happen? I know I am seated in authority in you, yet my words had no effect on him."

The Lord explained to me... "The enemy is a deceiver. He maintained an appearance as if your words had no affect on him but it was not the truth but in fact just the opposite. The truth is that every time you speak, things change in the spirit realm. The words you speak are powerful." The Lord continued... "The enemy does this, this deception, because he knows if he can hold on for only a short while, most believers will grow weary and give up."

I came to understand the power of the words we speak. This instruction from the Lord has proven to me over time, the importance of speaking the word of God over every area of life.

Why I Wrote This Book

I love to decree and speak over my life, my family, my work and every part of my life. I have seen the power of doing this and I know it has tremendous value. I talk to people every day who need breakthrough in their lives and need to know how it happens. Of course, we know the glory goes to the Lord for every good thing, but He gives us tools, covenants and promises that we are supposed to apply to our lives and circumstances. It is my desire that in explaining these things in the simplest way, those who read these words will apply and experience the power of the decree.

Heirs of God – Joint Heirs with Christ

We must first realize the role that identity plays when we speak of decrees, because any and all decrees we make are from that place of position in Christ. Our identity in Him is what gives us the legal right to do this regardless of what we are decreeing about. Whether decreeing over our families, finances, ministries, health, personal issues or anything else, our identity is what gives us the position to do this. We are legal heirs of the Kingdom of Heaven and as such, we have authority to use the name and position at the right hand of power in Christ Jesus.

1
OUR HERITAGE OUR VOICE

And God said, Let there be light: and there was light. (Genesis 1:3 KJV)

In the beginning we see God speaking things into existence. The very words He speaks cause things to be manifested and created. He is God after all. But we will see that He also instructs His children to speak things into being as well. (Ezekiel 37) Why wouldn't He? We are His after all and we are created in His image and likeness. Furthermore, not only did He create all things but He has given us dominion over the work of His hands.

For He spoke, and it was done; He commanded, and it stood fast. (Psalms 33:9 NKJV)

For I am the LORD. I speak, and the word which I speak will come to pass; it will no more be postponed; for in your days, O rebellious house, I will say the word and perform it," says the Lord GOD.' (Ezekiel 12:25 NKJV)

Ezekiel - Prophesy Upon These Bones

The hand of the Lord was upon me, and carried me out in the spirit of the Lord, and set me down in the midst of the valley which was full of bones,

2 And caused me to pass by them round about: and, behold, there were very many in the open valley; and, lo, they were very dry.

3 And he said unto me, Son of man, can these bones live? And I answered, O Lord God, thou knowest.

4 Again he said unto me, Prophesy upon these bones, and say

unto them, O ye dry bones, hear the word of the Lord.

5 Thus saith the Lord God unto these bones; Behold, I will cause breath to enter into you, and ye shall live:

6 And I will lay sinews upon you, and will bring up flesh upon you, and cover you with skin, and put breath in you, and ye shall live; and ye shall know that I am the Lord.

7 So I prophesied as I was commanded: and as I prophesied, there was a noise, and behold a shaking, and the bones came together, bone to his bone.

8 And when I beheld, lo, the sinews and the flesh came up upon them, and the skin covered them above: but there was no breath in them.

9 Then said he unto me, Prophesy unto the wind, prophesy, son of man, and say to the wind, Thus saith the Lord God; Come from the four winds, O breath, and breathe upon these slain, that they may live.

10 So I prophesied as he commanded me, and the breath came into them, and they lived, and stood up upon their feet, an exceeding great army.

Can you imagine if the Lord told you to speak to those bones? Do you have trouble believing for God to do the miraculous? What do we see here? Ezekiel did as the Lord commanded him. Obedience is a key to walking in the power of God and seeing miracles. We hear Him speak and we do as He instructs. Is anything too hard for God?

We know deep down inside that the words we speak make a huge difference in what comes to pass. We pray because we know this. We say certain things because we know this. We command devils to leave because we know this. We know His word is sharper than any two-edged sword. It isn't just God speaking or Jesus speaking but those He has given instruction to and told to speak. The works I do you shall do...

Joshua Commands the Sun to Stand Still

Then Joshua spoke to the Lord in the day when the Lord delivered up the Amorites before the children of Israel, and he said in the sight of Israel:

"Sun, stand still over Gibeon; And Moon, in the Valley of Aijalon." 13 So the sun stood still, And the moon stopped, Till the people had revenge Upon their enemies.

Is this not written in the Book of Jasher? So the sun stood still in the midst of heaven, and did not hasten to go down for about a whole day. (Joshua 10:12-13 KJV)

Elijah Calls Down Fire from Heaven

The fact that the bible mentions several times that Elijah called down fire, leads me to believe that this was something he was "walking in." Maybe he called down fire twenty times. One of the mistakes I believe people make is limiting the miracles of those days to what we have in a written record. Philip only translated one time? How do you know that? The bible says,

And there are also many other things that Jesus did, which if they were written one by one, I suppose that even the world itself could not contain the books that would be written. Amen. (John 21:25 NKJV)

My belief, drawn from the entirety of God's word, is that speaking and or decreeing miracles or miraculous events is not an anomaly but a lifestyle. It is a life lived unto God with His word being confirmed with signs following. The reason I like to share these stories of those who have gone before us is because we need to know this is normal, this is expected, this is something we need to accept and see manifest in our own lives.

So Elijah answered and said to the captain of fifty, "If I am a man of God, then let fire come down from heaven and consume you and your fifty men." And fire came down from heaven and consumed him and his fifty. (2 Kings 1:10 NKJV)

You understand this happened twice and was about to happen a third time until the last Captain got smart and pleaded with Elijah instead of trying to threaten him. Then we see again what happened on the Mount of Carmel.

36 And it came to pass, at the time of the offering of the evening sacrifice, that Elijah the prophet came near and said, "Lord God of Abraham, Isaac, and Israel, let it be known this day that You are God in Israel and I am Your servant, and that I have done all these things at Your word. 37 Hear me, O Lord, hear me, that this people may know that You are the Lord God, and that You have turned their hearts back to You again."

38 Then the fire of the Lord fell and consumed the burnt sacrifice, and the wood and the stones and the dust, and it licked up the water that was in the trench. 39 Now when all the people saw it, they fell on their faces; and they said, "The Lord, He is God! The Lord, He is God!" (1 Kings 18:36-39 NKJV)

One thing I want to point out here is that Elijah was saying "I have done all these things at your word." We can speak the word with boldness if we are under His authority and in obedience.

Joshua at Jericho

It shall come to pass, when they make a long blast with the ram's horn, and when you hear the sound of the trumpet, that all the people shall shout with a great shout; then the wall of the city will fall down flat. And the people shall go up every man straight before him." (Joshua 6:5 NKJV)

Now Joshua had commanded the people, saying, "You shall

not shout or make any noise with your voice, nor shall a word proceed out of your mouth, until the day I say to you, 'Shout!' Then you shall shout." (Joshua 6:10 NKJV)

So the people shouted when the priests blew the trumpets. And it happened when the people heard the sound of the trumpet, and the people shouted with a great shout, that the wall fell down flat. Then the people went up into the city, every man straight before him, and they took the city. (Joshua 6:20 NKJV)

This group was commanded first to march around the city for a week every day and then on the seventh day to march seven times before they shouted. Is this a decree? Not technically but they used their voice at the direction of the Lord and saw a miracle happen because of it. Can you imagine what people thought as they watched this opposing army march around their city? I bet they thought they were crazy. Often the Lord gives us instructions to follow that would cause non-believers to think we are not operating in the realm of reality.

The Lord once instructed me to march around our property seven times and then decree victory. I did it. What did the neighbors think? I have no idea and frankly do not care. I believing in obeying the voice of God regardless of what the world thinks or believes.

Speak to the Rock

Then the LORD spoke to Moses, saying, "Take the rod; you and your brother Aaron gather the congregation together. Speak to the rock before their eyes, and it will yield its water; thus you shall bring water for them out of the rock, and give drink to the congregation and their animals." (Numbers 20:7-8 NKJV)

Of course, we know that Moses did what God said up to a point. When the critical moment came, Moses struck the rock instead of speaking to it as God had instructed him. The rock

7

gave forth water but his own disobedience cost him. He was not allowed to bring the people into their promised land.

Have we seen enough examples to make my point? No. It isn't about making my point, it is about building faith to believe God will do this in and through you. You should research and study the scriptures and how God has led us to use our voice to speak things into being.

So then faith comes by hearing, and hearing by the word of God. (Romans 10:17 NKJV)

We create things with our words. We create and alter destinies with our words. We change the course of things with our words, in our own lives and in the lives of those around us. Don't get weird about this! "Are you saying we are like God now"? Only in the capacity that HE has given. Keep in mind that it is He who said "speak to the mountain," it wasn't something I came up with.

Jesus Gives the Instruction for a Miracle

When Jesus and the disciples were passing by the fig tree that Jesus had cursed, they saw it had dried up from the roots. "Look!" Peter had said. Jesus responded with something that pretty much should be the final word when talking about decrees or the power of the words you speak.

For assuredly, I say to you, whoever says to this mountain, 'Be removed and be cast into the sea,' and does not doubt in his heart, but believes that those things he says will be done, he will have whatever he says. (Mark 11:23 NKJV)

"Whoever shall say..."

Such as I Have

The disciples had come to understand who they were in Christ, or at least were coming into a powerful understanding.

We see this when Peter and John encountered the man begging at the Gate Beautiful.

Now Peter and John went up together to the temple at the hour of prayer, the ninth hour. 2 And a certain man lame from his mother's womb was carried, whom they laid daily at the gate of the temple which is called Beautiful, to [a]ask alms from those who entered the temple; 3 who, seeing Peter and John about to go into the temple, asked for alms. 4 And fixing his eyes on him, with John, Peter said, "Look at us." 5 So he gave them his attention, expecting to receive something from them. 6 Then Peter said, "Silver and gold I do not have, but what I do have I give you: In the name of Jesus Christ of Nazareth, rise up and walk." 7 And he took him by the right hand and lifted him up, and immediately his feet and ankle bones received strength. 8 So he, leaping up, stood and walked and entered the temple with them—walking, leaping, and praising God. 9 And all the people saw him walking and praising God. (Acts 3:1-9 NKJV)

They released what they had. They told him to get up and walk. It wasn't wishful thinking on their part. They were under authority and following orders. The result was a walking and leaping man who was praising God and giving him the glory.

It should not surprise us that we follow the Lord's instructions and do what He tells us to do and the result is a miracle. Why would that be surprising? This is about believing and obeying God. This is not about ministry appearance or pride or trying to look good or deceive someone. This is not even about doing this for any purpose of our own. This is about doing the will of the one who sent you. This is true, we know God honors His word.

Proving All Things

There are many. many more examples throughout the scriptures that show how the word spoken in the authority of Christ has wrought mighty miracles. I could provide them here for you but that defeats part of the purpose. You see, you must personally seek out the truth in scripture, being led of the Holy Spirit so that you will accept more readily what God shows you and so that it reinforces your commitment to be diligent to the work of the gospel.

We cannot place our trust in men, blindly believing what we hear when it comes to the things of God. Whether we are talking about salvation, healing, or the topic here, the power of decree.

The internet today has given us the ability to see and learn things that would have been near impossible in the past. We can see people heal the sick. On YouTube we can watch people get up out of wheelchairs as they are prayed over and told "rise and walk!" We can watch as people overcome with emotion have run around churches or meetings screaming "I'm Healed!" We can watch as people rebuke tornados in the name of Jesus and see the tornados turn and go away. We can watch people rebuke robbers and bandits using the name of Jesus and see them leave without incident. It's all there to see. We see Jesus in Matthew chapter eight rebuking the wind and waves. Does He still do this today? Maybe we should find out.

Jesus Rebukes the Wind and Waves

Now when He got into a boat, His disciples followed Him. 24 And suddenly a great tempest arose on the sea, so that the boat was covered with the waves. But He was asleep. 25 Then His disciples came to Him and awoke Him, saying, "Lord, save us! We are perishing!"

26 But He said to them, "Why are you fearful, O you of little faith?" Then He arose and rebuked the winds and the sea, and there was a great calm. 27 So the men marveled, saying, [b]"Who can this be, that even the winds and the sea obey Him?" (Matthew 8:23-27 NKJV)

There are people who have accepted Jesus as savior that

would rather rule these events as coincidence than say God did a miracle. Wake up people!

Get in the word of God and ask the HOLY SPIRIT to show you and lead you into the truth. He has promised to do it and He will. You can trust Him.

THE KING'S DECREE

2

DECREEING THE WORD OF GOD

What is a Decree?

According to several dictionaries, here are some of the most agreed upon meanings of the word "decree."

1.a formal and authoritative order, especially one having the force of law: a presidential decree.
2.In Law. a judicial decision or order.
3.In Theology. one of the eternal purposes of God, by which events are foreordained.
4.an official decision or order made by a leader or government
5.A royal decree is a decree given by a king or queen.

Explanation

If someone in authority decrees that something must happen, they decide or state this officially. In other words, decreeing is an announcement of sorts, carrying the force of law.

Royal decrees carry the force of law and are backed or enforced by the power of the kingdom they represent. For those who would decide to disobey or disregard the decree, they would find themselves jailed or worse. The power of the decree is a statement that says this decision will be carried out one way or the other, through willful or forced obedience. To me, this truth is both powerful and comforting.

We as believers make our decrees based on the highest power that exists and there is nothing greater that could even possibly overturn it.

Decrees can be written, spoken, or both.

Many times, decrees were written out with the royal seal attached to it as a record of the law or decision enacted. Sometimes the official spoken announcement would be made but also a copy of the decree would be posted in a public place so that all would know the law or rule that had been made.

When we make decrees as believers, the "royal seal" is the scripture we use or the word of the Lord we have been given. I say this because many times we speak to situations that are not spoken about directly in the bible but we can still decree and declare over those things at the leading of the Holy Spirit. Other times we may receive a prophetic word, or a word of instruction or encouragement from a prophet or someone who hears God's voice clearly. We can then speak or decree those things we have been given over our situations.

In my own life I have received several prophetic words and if they align with the heart of God and the word, I print them out into written form. I have them affixed to the wall next to my desk and I read them out loud and speak and decree them over my life.

We see in scripture the complete authority and power of God's word.

The Power of God's Word

In the beginning was the Word, and the Word was with God, and the Word was God. 2 He was in the beginning with God. 3 All things were made through Him, and without Him nothing was made that was made. (John 1:1-3 NKJV)

By the word of the LORD the heavens were made, And all the host of them by the breath of His mouth. (Psalm 33:6 NKJV)

Everything that was made was made through Him. He has complete dominion over all things.

He sent His word and healed them, And delivered them from their destructions. (Psalm 107:20 NKJV)

The word brings healing and deliverance.

We are told the word of God is powerful.

For the word of God is living and powerful, and sharper than any two-edged sword, piercing even to the division of soul and spirit, and of joints and marrow, and is a discerner of the thoughts and intents of the heart. (Hebrews 4:12 NKJV)

The Understanding and Faith of the Centurion

One of the greatest illustrations of the power of the word of God is shown to us in the book of Matthew chapter eight. In the town of Capernaum, we see Jesus is approached by a centurion who asks the Lord to heal his sick servant. When Jesus says "Yes, I will come and heal him" the centurion responds in this way...

8The centurion answered and said, Lord, I am not worthy that thou shouldest come under my roof: but speak the word only, and my servant shall be healed.
9 For I am a man under authority, having soldiers under me: and I say to this man, Go, and he goeth; and to another, Come, and he cometh; and to my servant, Do this, and he doeth it.
10 When Jesus heard it, he marvelled, and said to them that followed, Verily I say unto you, I have not found so great faith, no, not in Israel.
11 And I say unto you, That many shall come from the east and west, and shall sit down with Abraham, and Isaac, and Jacob, in the kingdom of heaven.
12 But the children of the kingdom shall be cast out into outer darkness: there shall be weeping and gnashing of teeth.
13 And Jesus said unto the centurion, Go thy way; and as thou hast believed, so be it done unto thee. And his servant was healed in the selfsame hour. (Matthew 8:8-13 KJV)

The story from the book of Matthew really gives us a clear lesson in speaking and declaring or decreeing something with the power and authority to back it up. The centurion explains to Jesus that he understands the rule of authority. He knows Jesus can speak the word and it will be done. He knows this because he also is a man under authority and when he speaks something it is done because of the authority that he is under. This is a huge key to your words carrying great power or no power. If we place ourselves under the authority of the Lord, that umbrella of power covers us. If we are in rebellion or disobedience to Him and His word then our words do not carry the seal of Heaven.

To have authority we must be under authority.

Forever, O LORD, Your word is settled in heaven. (Psalm 118:89 NASB)

Forever lets us know that this is not subject to change at some point and settled means that it is set in place, established and firmly fixed. Such is the absolute authority of the word of God. Therefor we know that His word carries power and authority but how is it that we as believers can also speak His word with the certainty of that authority?

Our Right to Decree God's Word

Through faith we understand that the worlds were framed by the word of God, so that things which are seen were not made of things which do appear. (Hebrews 11:3 KJV)

When we look at our right or ability or obligation to speak and declare or decree the word of the Lord, let me remind you again of the lesson from the book of Matthew. Obedience to God's word and His voice, placing ourselves under His authority is paramount to carrying the power of God in our mouths.

A Tragic and Sad Ending

I had a friend several years ago who had an incredible prophetic gifting. Just to "exercise" the gifts sometimes we would ask each other "What do you know?" about a person or situation that we knew nothing about in the natural. He could very often nail the situations by knowing the person's name, number of children, where they were from or born, and what the current issues they were facing. He could tell you about childhood traumas and at what age you suffered them. God had truly blessed him in this way.

When we first met many years ago, he carried incredible authority and power in his words. Evil spirits would literally cry out when they got near him, at church or in the grocery store. It was inspiring to me to see that level of relationship with God was possible today. Over the years however he fell prey to a twisted message of grace that taught that we could really live in any way we chose without being overly concerned because of the fact that there is "now no more condemnation to those who are in Christ." He began to make decisions that in my opinion were quite foolish especially for someone who desired to walk with God. It didn't happen overnight but over the course of ten years he was a different person. He still operated in a high degree of gifting but holiness and Christ-like character were no longer part of his discussion. There was still gifting but no power. If we do not come under His authority, we will not exercise authority.

By What Right do we do These Things?

What is the reason we decree, declare or speak the word of God over ourselves, our families, our lives and purposes? Why do we do it or why should we do it? Does it really have any effect?

Probably the most well-known scripture using the word decree is found in the book of Job.

Thou shalt also decree a thing, and it shall be established unto thee: and the light shall shine upon thy ways. (Job 22:28 KJV)

We are instructed to decree a thing but this authority is not from us.

Then He called His twelve disciples together and gave them power and authority over all demons, and to cure diseases. He sent them to preach the kingdom of God and to heal the sick. (Luke 9:1-2 NKJV)

And He said to them, "Go into all the world and preach the gospel to every creature. He who believes and is baptized will be saved; but he who does not believe will be condemned. And these signs will follow those who believe: In My name they will cast out demons; they will speak with new tongues; they will take up serpents; and if they drink anything deadly, it will by no means hurt them; they will lay hands on the sick, and they will recover." (Mark 16:15-18)

Then Jesus came and spoke to them, saying, "All authority has been given to Me in heaven and on earth. Go therefore and make disciples of all the nations, baptizing them in the name of the Father and of the Son and of the Holy Spirit, teaching them to observe all things that I have commanded you; and lo, I am with you always, even to the end of the age. Amen." (Matthew 28:18-20)

Jesus has delegated His authority to us and directed us to use it. I believe it is not just a right but an obligation. We are required to exercise His authority and release His power for the sake of the gospel. Knowing this, I believe we have the right to speak on His behalf and speak in the power of His authority over the issues of our lives or the lives of others.

The Power of our Decision

Many times, people get stuck at the starting gate of life because they don't have a clear idea of where they are going or what they are supposed to be doing. Many times, people don't see the breakthrough they need because they are asking amiss. What are we looking for? What really do we need to see come to pass? In the book of Job, it tells us to decide and decree a thing. Decide... make a decision. What do you want? What do you need? What is the voice of God saying to you? I believe we need to take this seriously. I have met people who spend more time deciding about vacation choices than they do the serious issues of life. Decide.

The NIV says this... What you decide on will be done, and light will shine on your ways.

The ISV says... When you make a decision on something, it will be established for you, and light will brighten your way. Here in the book of James it says this very clearly.

But let him ask in faith, with no doubting, for he who doubts is like a wave of the sea driven and tossed by the wind. 7 For let not that man suppose that he will receive anything from the Lord; 8 he is a double-minded man, unstable in all his ways. (James 1:6-8 NKJV)

I like what Joshua said...

And if it seems evil to you to serve the Lord, choose for yourselves this day whom you will serve, whether the gods which your fathers served that were on the other side of [a]the River, or the gods of the Amorites, in whose land you dwell. But as for me and my house, we will serve the Lord." (Joshua 24:15 NKJV)

Elijah also talks about making a decision.

And Elijah came to all the people, and said, "How long will you falter between two opinions? If the LORD is God, follow Him; but if Baal, follow him." But the people answered him not a word. (1 Kings 18:21 NKJV)

A decree is a decision made law; a line drawn in the sand. A decree is burning your bridge and saying this is the way its going to be. A decision with teeth. It us saying "No, I will no longer allow the enemy to steal our blessings" or "From this day forward I forbid the work of the enemy in the lives of my kids." It's saying "I will serve the Lord and Him only will I serve."

The Power of our Words

There are many scriptures that show either directly or indirectly the power of the words we speak. We remember from the book of Numbers chapter twenty the Lord told Moses to gather everyone together and speak to the rock and it will pour out it's water. We see by example that his words had power.

We also remember when Jesus rebuked the storm.

Then He arose and rebuked the wind, and said to the sea, "Peace, be still!" And the wind ceased and there was a great calm. (Mark 4:39 KJV)

But brother, that was Jesus! Surely (some will say) we can't do those things! Oh, to the contrary! As I mentioned before we not only can, but we are *expected* to do it. Jesus Himself said...

Verily, verily, I say unto you, He that believeth on me, the works that I do shall he do also; and greater works than these shall he do; because I go unto my Father. (John 14:12 KJV)

Indeed, there are many examples in the bible of words or speech carrying great power for the sake of the kingdom and the will of God. Use those examples as an encouragement for your own life.

Death and life are in the power of the tongue: and they that love it shall eat the fruit thereof. (Proverbs 18:21 KJV)

For verily I say unto you, That whosoever shall say unto this mountain, Be thou removed, and be thou cast into the sea; and shall not doubt in his heart, but shall believe that those things which he saith shall come to pass; he shall have whatsoever he saith. (Mark 11:23 KJV)

And whatsoever ye shall ask in my name, that will I do, that the Father may be glorified in the Son. (John 14:13 KJV)
A word fitly spoken is like apples of gold in a setting of silver. (Proverbs 25:11 ESV)

And the Lord shall utter his voice before his army: for his camp is very great: for he is strong that executeth his word: for the day of the Lord is great and very terrible; and who can abide it? (Joel 2:11 KJV)

We are ambassadors for Christ, representatives of the kingdom. Like our forefathers, the words we speak can carry great power. When I think of great examples for us to follow, Elijah stands out.

Elijah made a statement, a decree or a pronouncement or whatever you prefer to call it. He said to the captain...

And Elijah answered and said unto them, If I be a man of God, let fire come down from heaven, and consume thee and thy fifty. And the fire of God came down from heaven, and consumed him and his fifty. (2 Kings 1:12 KJV)

Notice that Elijah prefaced his decree with "if I be a man of God." He had an understanding that the power of his words did not come from himself, but rather from the God he knew and served. He recognized the relationship of his words and the kingdom he represented. This bears repeating for a reason. See yourself in this situation.

The third captain the king sent had more sense than to demand anything of Elijah but pleaded with him instead. He recognized the power that Elijah carried. Do people recognize that about us? Do people recognize that about you?

We understand that when we decree a thing, we are not randomly saying whatever pops into our head but are being led of the spirit as to what we speak. Even though the things we may decree over are very often the issues we are facing in our own lives, we are still led of the spirit in how to address them. Remember the words of the Lord...

Therefore, Jesus answered and was saying to them, "Truly, truly, I say to you, the Son can do nothing of Himself, unless it is something He sees the Father doing; for whatever the Father does, these things the Son also does in like manner." (John 5:19 NASB)

Can we really call down fire from Heaven or tell the sky to give no rain? Yes, by the spirit of God we surely can.

The Power of Negative Words

We can see by example many scenarios that show the power of God manifested through words. When it comes to warning about the power of negative words, we have many, many direct instructions in the scriptures. We are told over and again to guard our words and our tongue.

I think the wisdom here is even if we don't know how to speak or decree the word of God over our lives, at least we should know enough not to curse ourselves. The bible makes it real plain for us.

Let no corrupting talk come out of your mouths, but only such as is good for building up, as fits the occasion, that it may give grace to those who hear. (Ephesians 4:29 ESV)

I tell you, on the day of judgment people will give account for every careless word they speak, (Matthew 12:36 ESV)

When words are many, transgression is not lacking, but whoever restrains his lips is prudent. (Proverbs 10:19 ESV)

But now you must put them all away: anger, wrath, malice, slander, and obscene talk from your mouth. (Colossians 3:8 ESV)

Set a guard, O Lord, over my mouth; keep watch over the door of my lips! (Psalm 141:3 ESV)

The words of a whisperer are like delicious morsels; they go down into the inner parts of the body. (Proverbs 18:8 ESV)

How Long will you Falter Between Two Opinions?

How many times do we speak out against our own breakthrough or our own success? We spend months praying for God to move and then we say something like "It's never going to happen," or "If it was God's will it would have happened by now." Surely God realizes that we don't really mean it or we don't want the negative thing to happen. Yes, of course He does, but we need to realize that the words we speak are powerful.

God also realizes that as you drive your car, you didn't want it to go into the ditch but you have the right and the free will to steer it into the ditch if you choose to do it. We have the right and free will to choose the good thing or the bad thing. We have the ability to bless or curse with our words. Like the scripture says "set a guard over my mouth." We don't need to be cursing our own lives and families and blessings.

Keep your communication holy. Don't defile anything with your words.

Nothing breaks my heart more than to see parents "motivate" their children by saying hurtful or ungodly things to them. "You'll never amount to anything. Prove me wrong!" "You don't do it half as good as your brother (or sister) ." "You couldn't get a "A" if your life depended on it."

Many are only doing what was done to them and so it seems normal. We need a new normal. Reverse Psychology? That isn't the realm from which we operate. We decide and decree because we can. Speak only those things you actually want to see come to pass.

The Power of Words in the Spiritual Realm

One misunderstanding many have is that although it's not nice or not good to say negative things, it really isn't as bad as all that. The truth is that when we speak in agreement with our adversary the devil, we open a door to him. We give a permission of sorts for his involvement in our lives. Many don't believe that. "I am a believer and the enemy can't bother me no matter what." I have heard it said.

Do you not know that to whom you present yourselves slaves to obey, you are that one's slaves whom you obey, whether of sin leading to death, or of obedience leading to righteousness? (Romans 6:16 NKJV)

How does speaking against the will of God cause us to be a slave to the enemy? If the enemy tempts us in our thoughts to act or react in a way not pleasing to God and we do it, have we not obeyed the voice of the enemy? That's why the word tells us to take every thought captive. That's why the word tell us to think on those things pure and lovely and of good report. If we reject the voice of the enemy then we won't speak in agreement with the enemy. The power of life and death is in the tongue.

We should never let anything pass our lips that is in disagreement with God's word, not even as a joke or accidently. If we have done that we need to repent. We see television programs that talk about the self esteem of children and how the words of parents or other authority figures can either set them up for a grand life or destroy their lives. We think that this is because of the direct words and actions to the child. That is only a portion of the damage. The truth is that even words that the kids don't hear carry great power in the spirit to bring destruction. Spirits of rejection, rebellion, doubt, fear, worthlessness and inferiority ride on those words as surely as if the person knew they were pronouncing curses. It's kind of like those that say "I never do this (a particular sin) in front of the children because I wouldn't want to influence them". Well, I'm sorry to have to inform you that the minute you participate in a sin you have the potential to open that door to your family, whether they see you or not. So, whether you declare or speak something in a crowded room or alone in the middle of a forest, those words carry great power. We must learn to not just guard our words but realize we can change destinies with our words, for good or for bad.

Whose destiny would you like to see changed?

Also, please remember that our struggle is not flesh and blood. When we say negative words to someone it isn't just about hurting their feelings or discouraging them. There is a very real door in the realm of the spirit that gets opened. By our words we can grant access to the enemy and bring a spiritual mess into their lives. That is the weightier matter in speaking curses, whether intentionally or inadvertently. Our words affect both the natural and the spiritual realms.

Prophesy a New Destiny

A few years ago, a woman asked me to pray for her husband to come to Christ. She was very upset because she wanted to have a close relationship with him and with the Lord but as long as he was resisting the Lord, it was not possible. I felt compassion for her situation and began to pray.

The Lord stopped me after only a minute or so. "Prophesy a new destiny for him." The Lord said to me. I had never done that to my knowledge so I waited for the Lord to give me words. Soon the words began to flow. I spent the next few minutes declaring that the man was a mighty servant of the Lord and a powerful worshipper being used of god to bring souls into the kingdom and set the captives free. I don't remember everything I said, but I was speaking a life to him that was wholly redeemed. When the Lord said I was done, I stopped.

I again saw the same woman six months later at another meeting. She was weeping again but this time they were tears of joy. God had answered the cry of her heart and her husband had become all those godly things including becoming a powerful worshipper who was now leading worship in their church. That's the God we serve.

Decree Something to Build your Faith

So shall My word be that goes forth from My mouth; It shall not return to Me void, But it shall accomplish what I please, And it shall prosper in the thing for which I sent it. (Isaiah 55:11 NKJV)

I remember well one Saturday morning in late August the Lord speaking to me as I was praying and getting ready to go to work. I was bringing a rather big matter before Him and hoping to see Him move on our behalf. Suddenly the Lord said, "Decree this will come to pass." I heard it very clearly and it surprised me. "Lord, I'm not sure I have the faith for that." I said. "Lord, could I decree something smaller first to build my faith?" I felt the Lord was saying yes and so I did just that. I said, "I decree that it will snow here today and I will see it." Really? Snow in August? Well, it was late August and it was kind of a cool day. The bigger point was that it was easier for me to believe this kind of miracle than the one the Lord told me to decree.

I went to work and spent the day driving from one company to another, all the while keeping an eye on the sky for my snowfall. I looked with expectation most of the day and then without realizing it, I stopped watching the sky around five pm. I finished my work and began to drive home around six or so. Suddenly I began to see snow flurries coming down upon my truck. It came down heavy for about twenty seconds or so and I drove through it with my mouth open. I was in awe. With excitement, I said "No! I don't believe this is happening!" As soon as those words escaped my mouth, the snow stopped. I asked the Lord why it only snowed such a short time and He told me that was my doing. I had decreed it to happen and then spoke against it as it did. By my words the miracle was cut short. In Mark chapter eleven it tells us that whatever things you ask for and believe, will be yours.

I have had many people tell me that this miraculous weather was nothing more than a coincidence. I have heard that many times regarding many things that have been answers to prayer. All I can say is that when you have such a situation once, you have the right to call it coincidence. When "coincidence" happens every week, you should by then realize that God is still a God of miracles.

The point is that the Lord told me to decree a thing. It released His power. I have since decreed many things and seen many miracles. It should not surprise us that speaking the word of God or speaking in agreement with the word of God or obeying His instruction to speak, brings His kingdom to bear in our lives and situations. That is the whole point of His giving us all these things. Thy kingdom come.

3

PUTTING TOGETHER DECREES

The first thing many people wonder, is what areas of our lives are we able or allowed to make decrees over? Is there any area that is off-limits? Knowing that the Lord has great love for us gives us a clue as to this question.

He who did not spare His own Son, but delivered Him up for us all, how shall He not with Him also freely give us all things? (Romans 8:32 NKJV)

I believe there are two categories and these two categories cover between them all the issues of life. The revealed written word of God and the Rhema word of God are the two areas of which I speak.

The Written Word

The written word of God contains the will of God for our lives and circumstances. It carries the provisions and promises and covenants that we can depend upon. Although the written word does not specifically answer every question we may have, it does in a way because it tells us also how to get the specific answers we need. For example, the word does not tell you what color car you should buy but it does tell you that the Lord will supply all of your needs. If you need greater clarification than that, the Lord promises to give wisdom to all who ask for it.

The decrees that I speak over my own life and family and circumstances, I draw in part from the word of God, the bible. If we wonder what we can decree or what we may decree, the answer is found in God's revealed will. What is God's will for a certain situation? If you discover that, then you can have great confidence in what you decree based on His word.
For example...

Let's say I am in need of healing or am praying for someone else who is. What am I allowed to decree? What if there are issues that I don't know about? What if I don't see the whole picture? Very often, that will be the truth. You won't know the whole picture, but you can know the will of God.

As we look through the scriptures we see how Jesus dealt with those who needed to be healed. I would not only ask the Holy Spirit to highlight these scriptures to me, but also write them down so as to have a written record of the scriptures I am standing upon, or decreeing upon for this healing.

Scriptures of God's Will Concerning Healing

When evening had come, they brought to Him many who were demon-possessed. And He cast out the spirits with a word, and healed all who were sick, (Matthew 8:16 NKJV)

And when Jesus went out He saw a great multitude; and He was moved with compassion for them, and healed their sick. (Matthew 14:14 NKJV)

But when Jesus knew it, He withdrew from there. And great [a]multitudes followed Him, and He healed them all. (Matthew 12:15 NKJV)

Wherever He entered, into villages, cities, or the country, they laid the sick in the marketplaces, and begged Him that they might just touch the hem of His garment. And as many as touched Him were made well. (Mark 6:56 NKJV)

When we are talking about healing, I especially like Mark 6:56 because it shows really clearly that Jesus wasn't picking which He would heal. All who touched Him were healed.

Especially in the gospels we see many verses showing that Jesus healed those who came to Him. (Luke 4:40 / Luke 6:19 / Luke 9:11 etc.)

I have only listed a few scriptures here for the sake of example, but I would encourage you to really get in the word and find scriptures that talk about the areas you feel to speak the word of God over. Virtually every area of life you face has an answer in the word. Deliverance – Luke 10:17 / Resisting the devil – James 4:7 / Prosperity - 2 Corinthians 9:8 / Children – Isaiah 54:13 / Work or Job – Deuteronomy 28:12 / Protection – Psalms 91:11 / Hearing God's voice – John 10:27 / Being led of the Lord – Proverbs 16:9.

When we have the scriptures that the Lord has given us, we can use them to fashion a decree to speak to our own circumstances. That is the point of the Lord giving us the word, so that we might use it for our own lives. For instance using our example of healing I would take the scripture Matthew 8:16 and say "Lord you healed as many as came to you. I am coming to you and I thank you for healing me according to your word." Or Matthew 14:14 "Lord you are moved with compassion for those who are sick and I thank you for your compassion for me (or the one you are praying for) and I thank you for healing me."

As I am praying / decreeing this type of decree, where I am speaking to God, I also pray another type of decree where I am speaking to the sickness or the enemy behind the sickness. I believe this is very important as well and that is also why the word addresses this.

Then He called His twelve disciples together and gave them power and authority over all demons, and to cure diseases. (Luke 9:1 NKJV)

And when He had called His twelve disciples to Him, He gave them power over unclean spirits, to cast them out, and to heal all kinds of sickness and all kinds of disease. (Matthew 10:1 NKJV)
Let me add a couple other scriptures in here that may not immediately appear related.

Then God blessed them, and God said to them, "Be fruitful and multiply; fill the earth and subdue it; have dominion over the fish of the sea, over the birds of the air, and over every living thing that moves on the earth." (Genesis 1:28 NKJV)

But God, who is rich in mercy, because of His great love with which He loved us, 5 even when we were dead in trespasses, made us alive together with Christ (by grace you have been saved), 6 and raised us up together, and made us sit together in the heavenly places in Christ Jesus, (Ephesians 2:4-6 NKJV)

From these verses I would decree in this way...

"From my position in Christ, at the right hand of God, and because He has given me dominion over all things that move upon this earth, I decree sickness must go. I command all illness must go now. I take authority according to the word of God over everything that has brought sickness to my body and I command you leave now."

Be led of the spirit of God as you decree. He will give you the words to speak and you have to trust that. Also remember that this is not wishful thinking or "I hope this works", this is the truth of the word of God released over your situation. Remember the seventy who came back rejoicing because they discovered that the word they spoke had power and authority behind it.

Then the seventy returned with joy, saying, "Lord, even the demons are subject to us in Your name." 18 And He said to them, "I saw Satan fall like lightning from heaven. 19 Behold, I give you the authority to trample on serpents and scorpions, and over all the power of the enemy, and nothing shall by any means hurt you. 20 Nevertheless do not rejoice in this, that the spirits are subject to you, but [b]rather rejoice because your names are written in heaven." (Luke 10:17-20 NKJV)

Also, reminding you that the Lord told me sometimes the

enemy will try to resist, especially if he believes you are not convinced of the authority you have been given. Continue to decree anyway because the word is true. Don't let emotions direct you differently.

In my own life, my decrees have expanded through time as I have been led to new scriptures to include and given understanding concerning how they apply. You don't have to be an expert to decree a thing. Please remember that. God's provision during our learning curve is so far beyond what we can imagine it is profound. Many years ago, when I was first learning about deliverance, I was casting out a spirit from someone and called it by the wrong name as I commanded it to leave! Guess what happened? It came out anyway and never bothered the person again. If you think you have to be perfect or be an expert, think again. Thank you for grace Lord.

The Rhema Word

We can also make decrees based upon the rhema word of God, and sometimes the decree we speak is the rhema word of God. As we yield our tongue to the Holy Spirit, He can speak through us a rhema word. Rhema simply means "spoken word" in Greek. In the New Testament we see two ways that God speaks to us, the logos, which is the written word and the rhema, which is the spoken word. An example of the use of logos would be,

"In the beginning was the [logos] Word, and the Word was with God, and the Word was God" (John 1:1 NKJV).
An example of rhema would be,

"And take the helmet of salvation, and the sword of the Spirit, which is the [spoken] word of God" (Eph. 6:17 NKJV).

We can decree over a rhema word the Lord gives us either directly or through someone else. This idea of God speaking to us (rhema) is something that happens everyday and is not strange at all. Most of the time for most people we receive an impression in our minds or in our heart. If the Lord gives us something that we recognize and that means something to us we may value it enough to start speaking over it or praying about it or declaring it to come to pass. If we are given something that doesn't resonate with us or excite or interest us, we probably will not.

A Prophetic Word Confirmed

Several years ago, as I was just starting to learn what this meant, I received a powerful word from a prophet. The next day I received the same word almost verbatim from another prophet. At the end of that week I received the word again from another. It was a rhema word from the Lord that he confirmed through the mouths of three witnesses. I didn't know what exactly I should do but I knew I should do something.

I began to pray about this rhema word. I prayed Lord I receive whatever you are doing and I pray your blessing upon these plans. In my prayer, I repeated the word and prayed over each part, voicing my agreement with it and blessing upon it. I have seen this word unfold or come to pass in my life over these last several years and it has been quite an adventure. I honestly believe we have a choice though when God gives us a prophetic or rhema word. It is the choice we make that determines what happens next.

A rhema word from the Lord can change everything. He can tell you exactly how to pray for the sick or release healing. He can tell you the plans for your life, your family, your ministry or your work, and that specific word you receive can be the key, that unlocks the answer. It can literally change everything.

King David

If you really want to see someone decree and declare over their own life with great power, read the Psalms. The Lord placed something in David, something in his heart that was bigger than any opposition he faced.

"I will declare the decree: The Lord has said to Me, 'You are My Son, Today I have begotten You. 8 Ask of Me, and I will give You The nations for Your inheritance, And the ends of the earth for Your possession. 9 You shall [h]break them with a rod of iron; You shall dash them to pieces like a potter's vessel.' " (Psalms 2:7-9 NKJV)

But You, O Lord, are a shield for me, My glory and the One who lifts up my head. (Psalms 3:3 NKJV)

I will not be afraid of ten thousands of people Who have set themselves against me all around. (Psalms 3:6 NKJV)

I will both lie down in peace, and sleep; For You alone, O Lord, make me dwell in safety. (Psalms 4:8 NKJV)

What kind of prayer life did David had that this was the meditation of his heart? Out of the abundance of the heart the mouth speaks. You could very well highlight the majority of the Psalms to speak or decree over your life. Do you need faith? Hope? Strength? Trust? Boldness? It is all right there in the Psalms.

The Psalms? I thought we were talking about rhema, the Psalms are written. That is true but they were not written out so that David could read them, they were rhema to him. When God speaks to you in this way, be bold and declare the goodness of God. There are miracles waiting to be released.

Many times, the Lord will give you a word and then confirm it with a prophetic word. Perhaps the Lord has told you that He is going to send you to the nations, or maybe to specific nations like India and Indonesia. He has also told you that you are going to preach the gospel and heal many who are sick.

You can decree your agreement by saying "Lord, I thank you

for giving me India and Indonesia. I receive those nations and favor in those nations. I bless those nations and even now before setting foot there I bless the land and the people. I release healing virtue over those nations. I decree that many souls will be saved. I decree that many will be healed and restored."

Rhema words seem to tend to be more immediate, a word for now as opposed to a word for any time. For this reason, I believe they are important to be spoken or decreed as they are received. This is the answer for right now. That answer you need? This is it.

I remember about five years ago the Lord led me to pray for someone that was in a life or death situation. I didn't know what to pray or say or how exactly I was supposed to deal with it. I was torn in my heart because of the innocence of the life involved. I cried out to the Lord and He answered and gave me something to declare that solved everything. It was the word for that moment and the Lord gave it to me.

Another thing to keep in mind is that God can give you a word and you can also decree it in conjunction with the written word. I do this often. The Lord may give me a word to speak over someone's life and I am also very aware that I can do this because I am seated together with Christ. I am an ambassador of Heaven, a child of the most-high God. I am seated far above principalities and powers and many times I do not even feel led to speak it with my mouth but in my spirit.

I know who I am and to whom I belong. Period.

Make your Decrees

All those areas of life and family where you need to see breakthrough, begin speaking and decreeing the word and the promises of God over them. Prayer without ceasing is what the word says and I believe we can also say decree without ceasing until that breakthrough comes. Be diligent and be present. Be purposeful in this endeavor to decree the word of the Lord.
We must use wisdom. What could be wiser than speaking in agreement with the word of God? Make this an active part of your prayer life.

4

OUR IDENTITY IN CHRIST

The Importance of Identity

Our identity in Christ is paramount as we learn to decree and declare the promises of God over our lives and circumstances. It is from that position of our place in Christ that we even have the right to make these decrees and expect the power and authority of Christ to empower them or enforce them. Who we are, our identity is the reason we can decree a thing that it might be established and the light shine upon our ways. (Job 2:28)

The Lord spoke to me about identity many years ago when I was wondering if I was qualified to do the things I felt led to do and knew people needed me to do. I had a bit of an identity crises because I knew I was still a work in progress and the Lord had to give me some guidance over it. That's one of the important reasons we have to have and know our identity in Christ.

If you look around today you will see many people crying out for identity, crying out to belong somewhere. We see people dress certain ways or cut designs in their bodies or emulate and act like people on TV. It's all a desire to be valued, to belong, to have an identity of worth. If people don't know who they are they must search for an identity. Sometimes that identity is destructive and sometimes it is not but either way it is not the identity the Lord has for them. If their identity is not found in Christ, they have not found their true worth and true place.

Our Identity in Christ

Therefore, if anyone is in Christ, he is a new creation; old things have passed away; behold, all things have become new. (2 Corinthians 5:17 NKJV)

Ministry and Being Used of the Lord

I recently heard Rodney Howard-Browne say "in being used of the Lord, never let anyone tell you that you are unqualified. If you are saved, born again, you are qualified." That pretty much sums up the question of identity and our right or should I say privilege to be used of God. Not knowing, truly knowing one's identity keeps so many people from fulfilling the plan that God has for their lives. I have spoken to countless people who have told me that they don't feel qualified. They don't know enough scripture or they haven't been to bible college, some are still wrestling with sin issues or feel they are not a good enough example for God to use them. Some have been told by leadership in the church that God could never use them for various reasons. I've had more than one "apostle" tell me "quit telling people that God will use them like that. (in the gifts) You are giving them false hope. God uses those of us who have paid our dues so to speak."

I'm paraphrasing of course but many have been told they are not special enough to be used. We have to settle this. Jesus paid that price, so we didn't earn it. It is our identity in Him that qualifies us. We cannot take the glory because it doesn't belong to us.

This is one reason we need to know our identity and be secure in it. We need this to be established in us so that we can fulfill our call unhindered. This is why decreeing our identity every day is so powerful. We decree, we meditate on who we are, we praise and worship the Lord for what He has given us.

A Testimony

Many years ago, before I really understood what I was doing the Lord led me to say about myself what the bible says about me. In other words, to take passages from the word and declare them over or about myself. The word says we are supposed to heal the sick, so I would declare "I heal the sick." I wasn't saying I hope I can heal the sick. There's a difference. I would declare "I cast out devils" and "I walk in the freedom of the Holy Ghost." "I hear God's voice clearly." You get the idea. I wasn't really thinking about the scripture that says...

as it is written, "I have made you a father of many nations") in the presence of Him whom he believed—God, who gives life to the dead and calls those things which do not exist as though they did; (Romans 4:17 KJV)

You may say, "well this is talking about God not us'" and that would be true. The thing is that we have to remember that when we speak in faith over a situation it looks the same. We are saying things that those without faith definitely don't see and believing them to come to pass because of God's power working through us to fulfill His purpose. We know this to be true because of the examples the Lord gave us through teaching His own disciples about faith and prayer and calling things to happen without doubting in our hearts.

For assuredly, I say to you, whoever says to this mountain, 'Be removed and be cast into the sea,' and does not doubt in his heart, but believes that those things he says will be done, he will have whatever he says. (Mark 11:23 NKJV)

I don't know when exactly the shift took place but that became my life, healing the sick and casting out devils, walking in holiness and hearing God speak to me. There is power in decreeing a thing. When the Lord said "speak to the mountain", He meant it.

Obedience is Better than Sacrifice

In a time when I felt so unworthy the Lord told me to minister deliverance to someone. I resisted for about a week. My heart was breaking for the one who needed deliverance but I would not do it because I felt unqualified. Eventually, I obeyed the Lord and saw the person set completely free. It literally saved their life. They had been dying and the Lord set things right in that deliverance. God knows what He is doing. We have to believe Him and trust Him.

I started out by telling you that I didn't feel qualified nor did I consider myself to be qualified. I had to move forward in obedience to His voice. I argued with the Lord. "Lord I'm not worthy." He had to make me see that He has taken our sin and given us His righteousness, therefore we are worthy. For me to claim that I was not was saying that what He did was not enough to qualify me to be obedient to His instruction in the word.

Identity and Walking in Holiness

Who we are, or who we believe we are, plays a huge part in the way we act. The ideas and words we believe and the words we speak become as self-fulfilling prophecies. We act in agreement with the words we speak. What is in our hearts becomes manifest.

A good man out of the good treasure of his heart brings forth good; and an evil man out of the evil treasure of his heart brings forth evil. For out of the abundance of the heart his mouth speaks. (Luke 6:45 NKJV)

We see in the word that when we speak, we are really just releasing what is already there. The words we speak then bring an agreement and a strengthening of that thought or belief. If we took every thought captive, we would respond much differently. If an ungodly thought or an untrue thought presented itself, and we responded by saying "That's not true" we would not be fostering that untrue or ungodly thought.

..casting down arguments and every high thing that exalts itself against the knowledge of God, bringing every thought into captivity to the obedience of Christ, (2 Corinthians 10:5 NKJV)

Look at this scripture found in the book of Amos.

Can two walk together, unless they are agreed? (Amos 3:3 NKJV)

Our agreement will determine our walk. If we agree with the word and who the word says we are and who the word declares us to be, we will be walking in that. If we agree with the world, or the flesh or the devil, we will be walking a very different path. The point is that out of our agreement, or what we believe, our mouth speaks. As our mouths speak, we proclaim our agreement.

An Old Sinner

Years ago, in the church where I was raised, I heard a thousand times if I heard it once... "I'm just an old sinner saved by grace." It was considered a badge of humility and a means of giving the Lord all the glory and I'm certain that's how people meant it in their hearts. I know that when people made that statement (and I may even have said it myself) they were not trying to purposely declare they were still actively living in sin.

Many may think that this distinction is semantics. It is not. We need to be careful over the words we speak and the words we declare over ourselves and others. We know that if we have been saved, we are no longer "old sinners" but we are the redeemed of the Lord. We can't be both. When we were born again the Lord took our sin and gave us His righteousness. A more truthful and accurate statement would be "I was an old sinner but I have been saved by grace." Making the "sinner" part past-tense is the truth. To keep saying or declaring "I AM an old sinner" is not true or honoring to what the Lord did for us.

Further, it reinforces the idea in the natural and in the spirit that one is still a sinner, and what do sinners do? They sin. Therefor, when we do sin, (and according to First John we do)

If we say that we have no sin, we deceive ourselves, and the truth is not in us. (1 John 1:8 NKJV)

The explanation is simply "that is what normal behavior for a sinner is." It becomes a self-fulfilling prophecy and an excuse. It isn't that we mean for that to happen, but it is what the enemy is setting us up for.

We must know, understand and believe the truth and then speak that truth.

But God, who is rich in mercy, because of His great love with which He loved us, 5 even when we were dead in trespasses, made us alive together with Christ (by grace you have been saved), 6 and raised us up together, and made us sit together in the heavenly places in Christ Jesus (Ephesians 2:4-6 NKJV)

Wallowing in Sin's Memory

When I was first delivered from demonic oppression many years ago, I was overjoyed at the freedom that had been given to me. Nothing brings joy like freedom from oppression of the devil. I was new and I was clean. I felt clean and it was extraordinary. The one thing I did not immediately realize was that the sanctification of my soul had to be done. The Lord was not finished with me.

Many disagree with this. The idea is that when we are saved, everything is made right. The enemy has no place in your life anymore. That also, is not accurate. The enemy has no RIGHT to a place in your life. You still have to retake the land so to speak. Is this scriptural? Yes, here it is.

 When Jesus was speaking to the Samarian woman at the well in Matthew chapter fifteen, He said these words...

And He answered and said, "It is not good to take the children's bread and throw it to the dogs." (Matthew 15:26 NASB)

44

The woman was asking for deliverance for her daughter and Jesus said that was the children's bread.

Cleansing and purification, moving from glory to glory, is an ongoing situation.

Since you have in obedience to the truth purified your souls for a sincere love of the brethren, fervently love one another from the heart, (1 Peter 1:22 NASB)

As a practical example, we know many who get saved who are still addicted, still sick, still broke and still have bad habits. The difference is that now they have the power of God to address those issues and be conformed to His likeness.

For whom He foreknew, He also predestined to be conformed to the image of His Son, that He might be the firstborn among many brethren. (Romans 8:29 NKJV)

This is GOOD NEWS!

In my own life however, I was learning that even though I was indeed free, there were areas still that needed to come into agreement with my new life in Christ. It was a heartbreaking thing for me to realize. I felt horrible over my sin. I was seeing the reality of God's presence in my life and then I would fall in sin and I could not understand how it was possible.

Focusing on Sin

I would feel so badly that I would replay in my mind the sin I had committed, then I would allow guilt and shame to wash over me and then I would beat myself up over my lack of commitment to the Lord. I would listen to that voice that would tell me how unworthy I was and I would agree with that voice. "Yes. I am unworthy." I would allow this scene to play many times over several days before I would finally repent of my sins and ask forgiveness. The immediate problem was that I believed (falsely) that if I repented too quickly it would not be sincere. I was wrong.

I wrestled with this for a long time. Sometimes the truth of scripture, the instruction we should be following is right before our eyes but we overlook it to embrace some religious idea instead.

Old Identity

Herein lays the problem with focusing on "I'm an old sinner." It is our old, unsaved, unredeemed identity. I cried out to the Lord and He answered me. The Lord showed me that focusing on my sin or sins of the past was giving it access into my life. I was thinking that spending a few days replaying my sins and trying to bring to mind my own worthlessness was somehow a part of the repentance process. It isn't.

Brethren, I do not count myself to have apprehended; but one thing I do, forgetting those things which are behind and reaching forward to those things which are ahead, (Philippians 3:13 NKJV)

The Lord told me not to think about my old dead life, but meditate on who I AM now in Christ. In focusing on my old identity, I was focused on sin. The bible does not tell us to focus on sin or to think about sin. The bible tells us exactly the opposite.

When I would "repent" for several days, what kinds of things do you image I was saying? "I'm a mess." "I can't believe I did that." "I am so bad" , "I am so wrong."

New Identity

The Lord told me to repent immediately when I am first prompted to repent. Sometimes the call to repent came even as I was saying something I should not say! I didn't even have the words out yet and the Holy Spirit was telling me to repent! Then the Lord said to ask forgiveness and receive forgiveness and cleansing, and then forget it. We do not have the "luxury" of wallowing in the memories of our past sins.

If we confess our sins, He is faithful and just to forgive us our sins and to cleanse us from all unrighteousness. (1 John 1:9 NKJV)

"Forget the former things; do not dwell on the past. 19 See, I am doing a new thing! Now it springs up; do you not perceive it? I am making a way in the wilderness and streams in the wasteland. (Isaiah 43:18-19 NIV)

Therefore, if anyone is in Christ, he is a new creation; old things have passed away; behold, all things have become new. (2 Corinthians 5:17 NKJV)

It is biblical instruction to let go of the past.

Our True Identity

The Lord continued... not only stop meditating upon sin and declaring ungodly things over yourself, but begin meditating upon your true identity and decree and declare who you are over your life every day. The Lord led me to start my day, every day. Declaring my identity in Christ.

As I began to do this a funny thing happened, I was not struggling so much with sins I had previously been wrestling with. In the past it seemed as if I was walking a path and trying very hard not to look to the right or the left, but now I was walking in the opposite direction. It didn't matter if I looked right or left because the things I was trying to avoid were in the other direction and not on this new path. It was liberating. When you begin to walk in the fulness of who you are in Christ, new revelation flows and new mysteries unravel. The veils are no longer there.

A Vision from the Lord

Recently, I had a powerful vision that was a confirmation of something the Lord has now told me several times. Why did He have to tell me several times? I'm guessing because I was not doing as I was instructed.

As I was coming out of the vision and was at a place half between awareness and a fog, I heard the Lord ask me several questions. "Do you remember what I told you about declaring the things you want to see come to pass?" "Yes. Lord. I remember." I said. "Why do you not do it? You mention things in prayer yet do not contend using the revelation I have given you." He explained to me that it was if things mattered in the moment but not enough to keep pressing in when things grew a little easier.

The truth I know is that you can change your life or the lives of others through the words you speak. I know this. This is the reason I pray and decree and speak the word.

When we meditate on the word, believe it and declare it, then we are being conformed and transformed by the renewing of our minds, we are being washed by the water of the word and sanctified. Then, out of that abundance we speak and declare our agreement with the truth. We become strong in our identity.

Scriptures of Our Identity

You are Chosen

But you are a chosen people, a royal priesthood, a holy nation, God's special possession, that you may declare the praises of him who called you out of darkness into his wonderful light. (1 Peter 2:9 NIV)

just as He chose us in Him before the foundation of the world, that we should be holy and without blame before Him in love, (Ephesians 1:4 NKJV)

For whom He foreknew, He also predestined to be conformed to the image of His Son, that He might be the firstborn among many brethren. 30 Moreover whom He predestined, these He also called; whom He called, these He also justified; and whom He justified, these He also glorified. (Romans 8:29-30 NKJV)

You did not choose Me, but I chose you and appointed you that you should go and bear fruit, and that your fruit should remain, that whatever you ask the Father in My name He may give you. (John 15:16 NKJV)

For you are a [a]holy people to the Lord your God; the Lord your God has chosen you to be a people for Himself, a special treasure above all the peoples on the face of the earth. (Deuteronomy 7:6 NKJV)

You are an Heir

and if children, then heirs—heirs of God and joint heirs with Christ, if indeed we suffer with Him, that we may also be glorified together. (Romans 8:17 NKJV)

And if you are Christ's, then you are Abraham's seed, and heirs according to the promise. (Galatians 3:29 NKJV)

Therefore you are no longer a slave but a son, and if a son, then an heir [a]of God [b]through Christ. (Galatians 4:7 NKJV)

That having been justified by His grace we should become heirs according to the hope of eternal life. (Titus 3:7 NKJV)

He who overcomes [a]shall inherit all things, and I will be his God and he shall be My son. (Revelation 21:7 NKJV)

You are One with Him

but he who is joined to the Lord is one spirit with Him. (1 Corinthians 6:17 NKJV)

For in him dwelleth all the fulness of the Godhead bodily. 10 And ye are complete in him, which is the head of all principality and power: (Colossians 2:9-10 KJV)

Now, therefore, you are no longer strangers and foreigners, but fellow citizens with the saints and members of the household of God, (Ephesians 2:19 NKJV)

For He made Him who knew no sin to be sin for us, that we might become the righteousness of God in Him. (2 Corinthians 5:21 NKJV)

You are Light

Ye are all the children of light, and the children of the day: we are not of the night, nor of darkness. (1 Thessalonians 5:5 KJV)

For you were once darkness, but now you are light in the Lord. Walk as children of light (Ephesians 5:8 NKJV)

"While ye have light, believe in the light, that ye may be the children of light. These things spake Jesus, and departed, and did hide himself from them." (John 12:36 KJV)

Ye are the light of the world. A city that is set on an hill cannot be hid. Neither do men light a candle, and put it under a bushel, but on a candlestick; and it giveth light unto all that are in the house. Let your light so shine before men, that they may see your good works, and glorify your Father which is in heaven." (Matthew 5:14-16 KJV)

Arise, shine; For your light has come! And the glory of the LORD is risen upon you. (Isaiah 60:1 NKJV)

You are a Saint

Now, therefore, you are no longer strangers and foreigners, but fellow citizens with the saints and members of the household of God, (Ephesians 2:19 NKJV)

But fornication and all uncleanness or covetousness, let it not even be named among you, as is fitting for saints; (Ephesians 5:3 NKJV)

I now rejoice in my sufferings for you, and fill up in my flesh what is lacking in the afflictions of Christ, for the sake of His body, which is the church, 25 of which I became a minister according to the [a]stewardship from God which was given to me for you, to fulfill the word of God, 26 the [b]mystery which has been hidden from ages and from generations, but now has been revealed to His saints. (Colossians 1:24-26 NKJV)

giving thanks to the Father who has qualified us to be partakers of the inheritance of the saints in the light. (Colossians 1:12 NKJV)

Beloved, while I was very diligent to write to you concerning our common salvation, I found it necessary to write to you exhorting you to contend earnestly for the faith which was once for all delivered to the saints. (Jude 1:3 NKJV)

You have the Authority of Christ

But God, who is rich in mercy, because of His great love with which He loved us, 5 even when we were dead in trespasses, made us alive together with Christ (by grace you have been saved), 6 and raised us up together, and made us sit together in the heavenly places in Christ Jesus, 7 that in the ages to come He might show the exceeding riches of His grace in His kindness toward us in Christ Jesus. (Ephesians 2:4-7 NKJV)

Behold, I give you the authority to trample on serpents and scorpions, and over all the power of the enemy, and nothing shall by any means hurt you. (Luke 10:19 NKJV)

And Jesus came and spoke to them, saying, "All authority has been given to Me in heaven and on earth. 19 Go [c]therefore and make disciples of all the nations, baptizing them in the name of the Father and of the Son and of the Holy Spirit, 20 teaching them to observe all things that I have commanded you; and lo, I am with you always, even to the end of the age." [d]Amen. (Matthew 28:18-20 NKJV)

For the grace of God that brings salvation has appeared to all men, 12 teaching us that, denying ungodliness and worldly lusts, we should live soberly, righteously, and godly in the present age, 13 looking for the blessed hope and glorious appearing of our great God and Savior Jesus Christ, 14 who gave Himself for us, that He might redeem us from every lawless deed and purify for Himself His own special people, zealous for good works. 15 Speak these things, exhort, and rebuke with all authority. Let no one despise you. (Titus 2:11-15 NKJV)

And He called the twelve to Himself, and began to send them out two by two, and gave them power over unclean spirits. (Mark 6:7 NKJV)

And I will give you the keys of the kingdom of heaven, and whatever you bind on earth [a]will be bound in heaven, and

whatever you loose on earth will be loosed in heaven."
(Matthew 16:19 NKJV)

You are of God, little children, and have overcome them,
because He who is in you is greater than he who is in the
world. (1 John 4:4 NKJV)

You are a Son of God

Beloved, now are we the sons of God, and it doth not yet
appear what we shall be: but we know that, when he shall
appear, we shall be like him; for we shall see him as he is. (1
John 3:2 KJV)

For as many as are led by the Spirit of God, these are sons of
God. (Romans 8:14 NKJV)

You are a member of God's Household

Now, therefore, you are no longer strangers and foreigners,
but fellow citizens with the saints and members of the
household of God, (Ephesians 2:19 NKJV)

For you did not receive the spirit of bondage again to fear, but
you received the Spirit of adoption by whom we cry out,
"Abba, Father." (Romans 8:15 NKJV)

You are a Citizen of Heaven

For our conversation is in heaven; from whence also we look
for the Saviour, the Lord Jesus Christ: 21 Who shall change
our vile body, that it may be fashioned like unto his glorious
body, according to the working whereby he is able even to
subdue all things unto himself. (Philippians 3:20-21 NKJV)

You are / have the Righteousness of Christ

For He made Him who knew no sin to be sin for us, that we
might become the righteousness of God in Him. (2

Corinthians 5:21 NKJV)

But of Him you are in Christ Jesus, who became for us wisdom from God—and righteousness and sanctification and redemption... (1 Corinthians 1:30 NKJV)

For Christ is the end of the law for righteousness to everyone who believes. (Romans 10:4 NKJV)

You are a Dwelling Place for Holy Spirit

...in whom you also are being built together for a dwelling place of God in the Spirit. (Ephesians 2:22 NKJV)

Do you not know that you are the temple of God and that the Spirit of God dwells in you? (1 Corinthians 3:16 NKJV)

I will put My Spirit within you and cause you to walk in My statutes, and you will keep My judgments and do them. (Ezekiel 36:27 NKJV)

But if the Spirit of Him who raised Jesus from the dead dwells in you, He who raised Christ from the dead will also give life to your mortal bodies [a]through His Spirit who dwells in you. (Romans 8:11 NKJV)

You are Holy

But you are a chosen generation, a royal priesthood, a holy nation, His own special people, that you may proclaim the praises of Him who called you out of darkness into His marvelous light; (1 Peter 2:9 NKJV)

"For you are a [a]holy people to the Lord your God; the Lord your God has chosen you to be a people for Himself, a special treasure above all the peoples on the face of the earth. (Deuteronomy 7:6 NKJV)

And you shall be holy to Me, for I the Lord am holy, and have separated you from the peoples, that you should be Mine. (Leviticus 20:26 NKJV

*This verse tells us to "be holy" rather than you are holy. Can we still use this scripture in making our decrees? Yes, we can. First, we choose to be holy before God and then we may speak in agreement with it.

You are a King and a Priest

...and from Jesus Christ, the faithful witness, the firstborn from the dead, and the ruler over the kings of the earth. To Him who [a]loved us and washed us from our sins in His own blood, 6 and has made us [b]kings and priests to His God and Father, to Him be glory and dominion forever and ever. Amen. (Revelation 1:5-6 NKJV)

And have made us kings and priests to our God; And we shall reign on the earth." (Revelation 5:10 NKJV)

... you are a royal priesthood... (1 Peter 2:9 NKJV)

And you shall be to Me a kingdom of priests and a holy nation.' These are the words which you shall speak to the children of Israel." (Exodus 19:6 NKJV)

...you also, as living stones, are being built up a spiritual house, a holy priesthood, to offer up spiritual sacrifices acceptable to God through Jesus Christ. (1 Peter 2:5 NKJV)

You are an Overcomer and More than a Conqueror

Yet in all these things we are more than conquerors through Him who loved us. 38 For I am persuaded that neither death nor life, nor angels nor principalities nor powers, nor things present nor things to come, 39 nor height nor depth, nor any other created thing, shall be able to separate us from the love of God which is in Christ Jesus our Lord. (Romans 8:37-39 NKJV)

For whatever is born of God overcomes the world. And this is the victory that has overcome the world—[a]our faith. (1 John 5:4 NKJV)

You are of God, little children, and have overcome them, because He who is in you is greater than he who is in the world. (1 John 4:4 NKJV)

To him who overcomes I will grant to sit with Me on My throne, as I also overcame and sat down with My Father on His throne.(Revelation 3:21 NKJV)

Fear not, for I am with you; Be not dismayed, for I am your God. I will strengthen you, Yes, I will help you, I will uphold you with My righteous right hand.' (Isaiah 41:10 NKJV)

These are but a few of the many scriptures that reveal our identity in Christ and who we are to our God. As you search out scriptures on the thing which you desire to decree upon, make a substantial list. From the scriptures that the Lord has led me to, I will make my decrees and declarations.

Also please note that even though we may not decree all the scriptures every day, the words we speak are drawn from them and based upon them. I like to re-read them sometimes to reinforce the understanding that my decrees or my words have a solid foundation upon God's word.

My Decree of Identity in Christ

I am born again. I am cleansed and sanctified by the blood of Jesus Christ. My sin has been taken and I have the righteousness of Christ. I am holy before my God. I am of the family of God. I am an heir of God and joint heir with Jesus Christ. I am a legal heir of the Kingdom of Heaven.

I am a son of the most high God. I am seated in heavenly places in Christ at the right hand of God. I am seated in authority far above principalities and powers and my authority is in Christ, by His word, His name and His blood.
I am a new creation, created to do His will for His glory and I will accomplish those things by His almighty power. I am loved with an everlasting love and I am chosen of God. I am an overcomer and more than a conqueror through Jesus Christ.

I am king and priest and I submit myself to the king of kings to do His good pleasure. I will fulfill my purpose and calling in Christ,

Satan has no place in me and no power over me. I am free and filled with the Holy Spirit to the depths of my being. I am light as my Father in Heaven is light and there is no darkness in me.

I am one spirit with God and the works He does I will do also, for His honor and glory.

*Regardless of how I feel, or whether my emotions agree with these things in any given moment, all of these things are the truth, established by God, on my best days or even on my worst days.

Amen

Being Led of the Spirit

Because we are being led of the spirit, your decree may change even day to day. Some days you may feel to include something but not the next. That's ok. Just be led of the Lord as you decree over yourself the truth of God's word.

There are some days where I make these professions or decrees once in the morning and other days where I make them off and on throughout the day. Be led of the Spirit.

Worship and Thankfulness

The bible says...

Enter into his gates with thanksgiving, and into his courts with praise: be thankful unto him, and bless his name. (Psalm 100:4 KJV)

In addition to making declarations about our identity in Christ, I like to thank the Lord for this incredible blessing. I do this in much the same way I make the decrees, thanking the Lord for all of His blessings, provisions and covenants and for His goodness in providing these things.

A Prayer of Thanksgiving and Worship

Father, forgive my sins. Cleanse me from all unrighteousness. Make me clean and holy, sanctified so that you might use me mightily for your glory.

I thank you for all you have done. I thank you for my salvation. I thank you that Jesus paid the price for me. I praise you for your faithfulness and I praise you for your provision.

I thank you that you have chosen me and made me an heir and joint-heir with Christ. I thank you and praise you that I am one spirit with you.

I praise you that you have seated me in authority in heavenly places in Christ and that nothing by any means will harm me. I thank you Father that I am a son of God and I am led by your spirit.

I praise you that I am but a sojourner here in this world but a member of your own household and a citizen of Heaven.

Thank you that you have taken away my sin and given me your righteousness. I thank you that you have filled me with your Holy Spirit and made me holy.

Thank you Father, that you have made me both king and priest to rule and reign under your authority over all those things you have entrusted to me. That your kingdom may come and your will is done.

I praise you and thank you for making me an overcomer by your almighty hand and I yield to your will in all these things. Thank you Father. Thank you Lord and thank you Holy Spirit.

Amen.

A brief word about this prayer. This prayer of thankfulness and praise is also a prayer of petition as well. As we thank Him we are making our desires known that we want to be in His will, and accept His will for our lives.

The bible tells us...

Be anxious for nothing, but in everything by prayer and supplication, with thanksgiving, let your requests be made known to God; (Philippians 4:6 NKJV)

May the Lord bless you and keep you.

More Resources

This book is a very small resource concerning decrees. The truth is that I am a very "nuts and bolts" type writer. I like to provide the essential tools to get the job done and believe that you will dig into the scriptures to find more. It is my desire to give something that you can use today and not something you have to study for month and still must figure out for yourself. In the very near future I will provide some additional and specific materials with examples and explanations of decrees over the areas of Our Identity in Christ and other areas as well. These books will have decrees written out fully with explanations as to the importance of these areas of decree so please look for them.

About the Author

Michael Van Vlymen is a writer and speaker who teaches about the miraculous things of God. Michael with his wife Gordana travel throughout the world teaching, imparting and equipping the saints to walk in the fullness of their calling. Their ministry is called River of Blessings International Ministries and is based in Carmel, Indiana USA.

www.riverofblessingsinternationalministries.org

THE KING'S DECREE

Printed in Great Britain
by Amazon

47034121R00040